Procuring Penetration Testing Services

Procuring Penetration Testing Services

Warning

This Guide has been produced with care and to the best of our ability. However, CREST accepts no responsibility for any loss, damage or incidents arising from its use from any cause whatsoever.

Every possible effort has been made to ensure that the information contained in this book is accurate at the time of going to press, and the publisher and the author cannot accept responsibility for any errors or omissions, however caused. Any opinions expressed in this book are those of the author, not the publisher. Websites identified are for reference only, not endorsement, and any website visits are at the reader's own risk. No responsibility for loss, damage or incidents occasioned to any person acting, or refraining from action, as a result of the material in this publication from any cause whatsoever can be accepted by the publisher or the author.

Apart from any fair dealing for the purposes of research or private study, or criticism or review, as permitted under the Copyright, Designs and Patents Act 1988, this publication may only be reproduced, stored or transmitted, in any form, or by any means, with the prior permission in writing of the publisher or, in the case of reprographic reproduction, in accordance with the terms of licences issued by the Copyright Licensing Agency. Enquiries concerning reproduction outside those terms should be sent to the publisher at the following address:

IT Governance Publishing
IT Governance Limited
Unit 3, Clive Court
Bartholomew's Walk
Cambridgeshire Business Park
Ely, Cambridgeshire
CB7 4EA
United Kingdom
www.itgovernance.co.uk

The author has asserted the rights of the author under the Copyright, Designs and Patent Act, 1988, to be identified as author of this work.

First published in the United Kingdom in 2014

by IT Governance Publishing

ISBN 978-1-84928-575-9

TABLE OF CONTENTS

INTRODUCTION

Organisations like yours have the evolving task of securing complex IT environments whilst delivering their business and brand objectives. The threat to key systems is ever increasing and the probability of a security weakness being accidentally exposed or maliciously exploited needs to be continually assessed – *such as via a penetration test* – to ensure that the level of risk is at an acceptable level to the business.

A penetration test involves the use of a variety of manual and automated techniques to simulate an attack on an organisation's information security arrangements – either from malicious outsiders or your own staff.

Undertaking a series of penetration tests will help test your security arrangements and identify improvements. When carried out and reported properly, a penetration test can give you knowledge of nearly all of your technical security weaknesses and provide you with the information and support required to remove or reduce those vulnerabilities. Research has shown that there are also other significant benefits to your organisation through effective penetration testing, which can include:

- A reduction in your ICT costs over the long term;
- Improvements in the technical environment, reducing support calls;
- Greater levels of confidence in the security of your IT environments;
- Increased awareness of the need for appropriate technical controls.

Many organisations choose to appoint a trusted, specialist organisation (a CREST member), employing qualified professionals (CREST qualified staff), to help them conduct penetration tests. Although these suppliers are sometimes employed just to conduct testing, they can also help you when specifying requirements, defining the scope of the test and developing a management framework.

Penetration testing is not, however, a straightforward process – nor is it a panacea for all ills. It is often very technical in nature, and the methods used and the output can be riddled with jargon, which can be daunting for organisations considering the need for it. Furthermore, buyers have reported a number of difficulties when conducting penetration tests, which include:

- Determining the depth and breadth of coverage of the test;
- Identifying what type of penetration test is required;
- Managing risks associated with potential system failure and exposure of sensitive data;
- Agreeing the targets and frequency of tests;
- Assuming that by fixing vulnerabilities uncovered during a penetration test, their systems will then be 'secure'.

To help address these issues, a research project was commissioned by CREST to produce a *Procurement Guide for penetration testing services,* addressing the main requirements organisations have for considering and conducting penetration tests.

⊘ One of the main reasons for commissioning a research project was that the potential customers of CREST members were often unclear about how to best procure penetration testing services.

Penetration testing is typically deployed to gain an assessment of IT infrastructure, networks and business applications to identify attack vectors, vulnerabilities and control weaknesses. It involves an active analysis of the target system for any potential vulnerabilities that could result from poor or improper system configuration, both known and unknown hardware or software flaws, and operational weaknesses in process or technical countermeasures.

⊘ Penetration testing looks to exploit known vulnerabilities but should also use the expertise of the tester to identify specific weaknesses – unknown vulnerabilities – in an organisation's security arrangements.

Penetration testing should be placed in the context of security management as a whole. To gain an appropriate level of assurance, a range of reviews should be conducted. These are often aligned to standards such as ISO27001, COBIT or the ISF Standard of Good Practice. Whilst these standards reference penetration testing, they only do it from a management perspective – and systems that comply with these standards may not be technically secure. A balanced approach of technical and non-technical testing should therefore be taken to ensure the overall integrity of security controls.

⊘ While other forms of security assurance provide only a theoretical articulation of vulnerability, penetration testing demonstrates actual vulnerability against defined and real threats. As such the results from a penetration test can be more compelling and demonstrable to both senior management and technical staff.

'Organisations should not describe themselves as secure – there are only varying degrees of insecurity.'

A STRUCTURED APPROACH TO PENETRATION TESTING

When performing penetration tests, some organisations adopt an ad hoc or piecemeal approach, often depending on the needs of a particular region, business unit – or the IT department. Whilst this can meet some specific requirements, this approach is unlikely to provide real assurance about the security condition of your systems enterprise-wide. Consequently, it is often more effective to adopt a more systematic, structured approach to penetration testing, ensuring that:

- Business requirements are met;
- Major system vulnerabilities are identified and addressed;
- Risks are kept within business parameters.

To help you make the most of your penetration testing, a procurement approach has been developed and is presented on the following page. The five stages in this approach involve determining business requirements; agreeing the testing scope; establishing a management framework (including contracts, risk, change and problem management); planning and conducting the test itself and implementing an effective improvement programme.

A: Determine business requirements for a penetrations test, considering the:
* Drivers for testing, such as compliance, serious (often cyber-related) incidents, outsourcing, significant business changes and the need to raise security awareness
* Target environments to be tested, such as critical or outsourced business applications (and infrastructure), or those under development
* Purpose of testing (eg to identify weaknesses in controls, reduce incidents and comply with legal, regulatory or customer requirements.

E: Implement an improvement programme to:
* Address weaknesses, including root causes, evaluating potential business impact
* Evaluate penetration testing effectiveness, to help determine if objectives were met and that value for money has been obtained from your supplier
* Identify lessons learned, and record them, to help avoid weaknesses recurring
* Apply good practice, beyond the target, across a wide range of other environments
* Create an action plan, to ensure remedial actions are prioritised, allocated to accountable individuals and monitored against target dates for completion
* Agree an approach for future testing, considering results from previous tests.

Procure penetration testing services

B: Agree the testing scope, which includes:
* Approving the testing style (eg black box, where no information is provided to testers; white box, where full access is provided; or grey box, somewhere in between)
* Determining the type of testing to be done, such as web application or infrastructure
* Assessing test constraints, due to legal, operational, timing of financial requirements.

D: Plan and conduct the penetration test itself, which consists of:
* Developing a detailed test plan that identifies the processes, techniques or procedures to be used during the test.
* Conducting research, analysing information and performing reconnaissance
* Identifying vulnerabilities (eg technical vulnerabilities or control weaknesses)
* Exploiting weaknesses (eg to gain authorised access)
* Reporting key findings, in an agreed format in both technical and business terms
* Remediating issues, addressing identified vulnerabilities and associated 'root causes'.

C: Establish a management assurance framework to:
* Assure the quality of penetration testing, monitoring performance against requirements
* Reduce risk (eg degrading or loss of services; disclosure of sensitive information)
* Manage changes (eg to the testing scope or to the configuration of the target system)
* Address problems, using a problem resolution process, to ensure that any issues are resolved satisfactorily, in a timely manner
* Agree scope, defined in a legally binding contract, signed by all parties prior to testing.

CHOOSING A SUITABLE SUPPLIER

Organisations can carry out penetration testing themselves, sometimes very successfully. More often they will decide to employ the services of one or more specialist third party penetration testing providers.

Findings from the research project indicated that the main reasons why organisations hire external suppliers are because these suppliers can:

1. Provide more experienced, dedicated technical staff who understand how to carry out penetration tests effectively, using a structured process and plan;
2. Perform an independent assessment of their security arrangements;
3. Carry out a full range of testing (eg black, white or grey box; internal or external infrastructure or web application; source code review; and social engineering);
4. Conduct short term engagements, eliminating the need to employ your own specialised (and often expensive) technical staff.

'We suspected that we had already been hacked and wanted to find out more about the threats to our systems, to help reduce the risk of another successful attack.'

When appointing an external provider of penetration services, it is important that you choose a supplier who can provide a reliable, effective and proven penetration testing service – but at the right price. To do this, it can be useful to:

1. review requirements;
2. define supplier criteria;
3. appoint appropriate supplier.

A. Review requirements

The first step is to make sure that whoever chooses the supplier (preferably not just a procurement specialist) fully understands your organisation's requirements, and is aware of any necessary management, planning and preparation activities.

◉ There are many benefits in procuring penetration testing services from a trusted, certified external company who employ professional, ethical and highly technically competent individuals. CREST member companies are certified penetration testing organisations that fully meet this requirement, have been awarded the gold standard in penetration testing and build trusted relationships with their clients.

'Our supplier is a trusted organisation who employs competent people – and this combination is important'

B. Define supplier selection criteria

To ensure that your chosen supplier will meet your requirements it can be helpful to define a set of supplier criteria, most of which your chosen supplier should be able to meet – or exceed. The six main criteria identified during the research project are outlined on the following pages together with examples of the types of questions you may wish to consider as part of the selection process.

'A good supplier helps to assure the process for a proper security test without creating misunderstandings, misconceptions, or false expectations.'

Selection criteria 1 – Solid reputation, history and ethics

Typical questions to ask a potential supplier	Comments
a. Can you provide evidence of a solid reputation, history and ethics (eg. a full trading history; good feedback from both clients and suppliers; a reliable financial record; and a strong history of performance)?	Two of the most important criteria for a buyer of penetration testing services to consider are the reputation (and history) of the supplier; and the ethical conduct they both adopt and enforce.
b. Do you take part in specialised industry events (such as those run by CREST or OWASP chapters)?	A reputable supplier will have achieved suitable professional accreditation (such as CREST), and be a member of current, relevant professional and industry bodies.
c. Are you able to demonstrate exploits or vulnerabilities you have found in other similar environments?	
d. Can you provide independent feedback on the quality of work performed and conduct of staff involved?	They will also have processes in place for agreeing scope and obtaining permissions for the type of work to be conducted, where it will take place and what information and systems will be accessed.
e. Do you adhere to a formal code of conduct overseen by an independent industry body?	

Selection criteria 2 – High quality, value-for-money penetration testing services

Typical questions to ask a potential supplier	Comments
a. Can you show that you provide high quality services, including the methodologies, tools, techniques and sources of information you will use as part of the testing process?	Some suppliers will hit you with a volley of 'vendor hype' that can be difficult to penetrate. It can therefore be a real challenge to find the right quality of service at the right price.
b. How do you perform rigorous and effective penetration tests to ensure that a wide range of system attacks are simulated?	Suppliers should be able to produce insightful, practical and easy to read reports, engaging with senior management in business terms, resolving issues with IT service providers, and addressing global risk management issues.
c. Can you describe your proven testing methodology that is tailored for particular types of environment (eg. infrastructure, web applications, mobile computing)?	
d. Can you demonstrate your organisations' penetration testing capabilities (eg. by make a presentation; showing examples of similar (sanitised) projects they have undertaken) and providing a sample report?	A quality supplier will not only deliver a highly effective testing process, but can differentiate themselves by the quality of the customer services they provide, effectively providing a professional service wrapper around the test.
e. Do you have independently reviewed quality assurance processes that apply to each test being undertaken, to help make sure client requirements are being met in a secure, productive manner?	

'If you have been compelled to conduct a penetration test, then our penetration testing services may not be for you, but if you want to conduct a proper test, give us a call.'

Selection criteria 3 – Research and development capability

Typical questions to ask a potential supplier	Comments
a. Do you have an active, continuous and relevant research and development capability? b. Have you produced research papers, published vulnerabilities or won awards in the industry? c. Do you perform sufficient research and development to be able to identify all significant vulnerabilities? d. How do you carry out specially tailored, manual tests to help detect unknown vulnerabilities, rather than just using a standard set of tools?	One of the biggest selling points for some suppliers is the quality and depth of their technical research and development (R&D) capability. Some suppliers will constantly develop specific methodologies to address different environments, such as infrastructure, web application, wireless, mobile etc. A good technically competent supplier is likely to carry out about 70% manual testing (simulated hacking!), as opposed to 30% using automated tools.

Selection criteria 4 – Highly competent, technical testers

Typical questions to ask a potential supplier	Comments
a. What qualifications do your testing staff hold in the various areas in which tests may be required (such as web application testing)?	The penetration testers used by your supplier should have deep, technical capabilities in the specific areas that are relevant to your target environment (eg web application, infrastructure, mobile or vendor-specific).
b. How do your testers identify 'root cause' findings, strategically analyse findings in business terms, help develop security improvement strategies and recommend countermeasures to both address vulnerabilities and prevent them recurring?	CREST provides accreditation in different technical areas, such as CREST web application testers and CREST infrastructure testers. There are also specific examinations in areas such as wireless testing.
c. Can you specify: named individuals who will be responsible for managing and conducting the test, their experience of the environment within the scope, their qualifications and the exact role each individual will perform?	

'Put the right people from the right organisation on the right job at the right time'

Selection criteria 5 – Security and risk management

Typical questions to ask a potential supplier	Comments
a. Do you apply independently validated security and risk management controls over the testing process, all relevant people involved, key aspects of target systems and any client data affected? b. Can you provide written assurances that the security and risks associated with our critical systems and confidential information (together with any other business risks) will be adequately addressed – and compliance requirements met? c. How do you ensure that results of tests are generated, reported, stored, communicated and destroyed in a manner that does not put the organisation at risk?	It is important that the supplier themselves is secure – and has a positive approach to both security and risk. Your supplier should be able to provide assurances – preferably in writing – that the security and risks associated with your critical systems and confidential information (together with any other business risks) are being adequately addressed. During any security assessment it is likely that the test team will encounter sensitive or business critical data. You will need to be comfortable that you can trust both the supplier – and every individual tester they provide.

Selection criteria 6 – Strong professional accreditation and complaint process

Typical questions to ask a potential supplier	Comments
a. Does your organisation hold strong professional accreditation? b. Can you outline the problem reporting and escalation processes that you adopt should there be a problem with the testing? c. Are you supported by a constructive, expert complaint process, with sufficient independence and authority to resolve issues?	Penetration testing organisations who have been professionally accredited will provide you with confidence that major vulnerabilities have been identified and properly addressed. They will also bring with them a wealth of experience drawn from client work across a range of companies and sectors, allowing lessons learnt from one to be transferred to others. The CREST scheme requires organisations to demonstrate that they have appropriate procedures and controls in place to protect client information and systems.

There can be a big difference between a cheap penetration testing service and one that provides real value for money. For example, many low cost services may not provide certified, professional staff that can uncover and address significant vulnerabilities or act in an ethical manner according to a defined code of conduct. Furthermore, there is typically little recourse in the event of a dispute (eg. no independent adjudication and sometimes not even any indemnity insurance).

'CREST provides demonstrable assurance of the processes and procedures of member organisations and validates the competence of information security testers.'

C. Appoint appropriate supplier

It can often be difficult to produce a short list of potential suppliers, not least because there are so many to choose from. For example, penetration testing suppliers can include:

- Organisations specialising in penetration testing (often small boutique firms) – who may have specialist research and testing capabilities;
- Information security consultancies and integrators, with penetration testing teams – who may have wider links to information security strategy and integration with security management standards;
- Systems integrators and outsourcing service providers with penetration testing teams – who may have detailed understanding of your technical environment and knowledge of attacks to similar outsourced organisations;
- Regulated professional services firms, including the 'Big 4' accountancy firms, with penetration testing teams – who may be more heavily regulated, with links to wider audit and compliance requirements.

✅ Although value can be obtained by appointing either certified testers or certified organisations, it is the combination of these that will provide you with the greatest assurance that the most effective tests will be conducted – and in the most professional manner.

By procuring penetration testing services from certified testers who work for certified organisations (as CREST require), you can rest assured that an expert and independent body – with real authority – is on hand to investigate any complaint thoroughly and ensure that a satisfactory conclusion is reached.

After carefully considering all the relevant supplier selection criteria – and evaluating potential suppliers – you will then need to formally appoint one or more suppliers. The key consideration should still be to select a supplier who can help you meet your specific requirements – at the right price – not just one who can offer a variety of often impressive products and services, some of which may not necessarily be relevant.

● Tests are often carried out on a regular (typically annual) basis. However, they are often more effective if carried out immediately before (or after) a major change – often saving money in the longer run, too.

'It is important to ensure that the right systems are being tested by the right people for the right reasons at the right time'

SUMMARY

Like many others, your organisation can benefit from conducting effective, value-for-money penetration testing. To achieve this, you will need to plan for a penetration test, select an appropriate third party provider, and manage all important related activities.

Firstly, there are a number of key concepts you will need to understand to conduct a well-managed penetration test, such as understanding what a penetration test is (and is not), appreciating its' strengths and limitations, and considering why you would want to employ an external provider of penetration testing services.

Secondly, to ensure requirements are satisfactorily met, it is advisable to adopt a systematic, structured approach to penetration testing. This involves determining business requirements; agreeing the testing scope; establishing a management framework (including contracts, risk, change and problem management); planning and conducting the test itself; and implementing an effective improvement programme.

Finally, if your organisation decides to appoint an external provider of penetration services, it is important that you choose a supplier who can most effectively meet your requirements – but at the right price. It is often helpful to determine a set of criteria when choosing an appropriate supplier, considering the six key selection criteria outlined in this report.

⊘ A useful set of presentation slides has also been produced, summarising the main findings from the project and including all the diagrams. Both this and the full Procurement Guide are available from CREST at www.crest-approved.org/

'What we are looking for from a supplier is certainty, prioritisation, trust and security'

CREST BALANCED SCORECARD

Company Membership

Demonstrable level of assurance of processes and procedures of member organisations.

Knowledge Sharing

Guidance and standards. Opportunity to share and enhance knowledge.

Professional Qualifications

Validate the competence of information security professionals.

Professional Development

Encourage talent into the market. On-going personal development.

For further information contact CREST at *www.crest-approved.org*

EU for product safety is Stephen Evans, The Mill Enterprise Hub, Stagreenan, Drogheda, Co. Louth, A92 CD3D, Ireland. (servicecentre@itgovernance.eu)

www.ingramcontent.com/pod-product-compliance
Lightning Source LLC
Chambersburg PA
CBHW070907070326
40690CB00009B/2029